MICHELLE'S B

FIYA

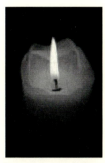

In all we do, the fire is lit
The candle burn
Hatred stirs
Take fold
Become thought
Burns our thoughts
Consumes us
Evolve
Takes shape

We react
Talk shit
Lay the blame
We become insane; incensed
The destroyer and destroyed
Killed

Michelle

Book 22 of the Michelle's Book Blog Series wow.

I am so going to get right into this book because I am hoping this book will be truly short and sweet and yes brutally honest and true. I will try to stay away from politics because politics is a death trap from me and the messengers of Lovey; Good God and Allelujah.

Further, if I do not have 32 pages by the time I am done, I am going to add fillers to make up the 32 pages I need to upload this book on Lulu.

__Now Foota Hype wow. Yu get mi to claate but let it be over because I am not buying your UFO bullshit.__

I will not disclaim your stroke but come on now, your UFO crap. Dimensional travel is possible yes, but come on now. Do not go there because __*I KNOW, NO JUDGE CAN CHARGE A MAD MAN FOR INSANITY. ALL DEM CAN DU A LOCK DEM UP INNA MAD HOUSE.*__

People, my true family, it is unethical for a judge to lock up a mad man; meaning put them in prison because they are not of a sound mind. They are not acting on their own behalf thus they are delusional. __And it matters not if Science is involved.__

Foota Hype yu nuh mad.
You are not delusional.

You are of sane and or sound mind and thought including thoughts. So truly stop it because all that you do is premeditated. You can fool di Jamaican people dem but you cannot fool me; thus let the anger and feud go. It is not warranted because the both of you are done. Let her go because I know what you are doing and you are sane. All that you do is thought of and premeditated.

She did move on without you. All the plans you made backfired and she is living her life. You must live your life now and think of your child with her.

No man has control over a woman.

No man has the right to abuse a woman. When you do this, you have no respect for her as woman nor do you respect her as the mother of your child. In all that you do, you do not respect the womb of life nor do you respect the woman and or mother that gave birth to you.

When you beat your wife and girlfriend it's like beating your own mother. And in fact you are. You are beating your own mother because you are disrespecting life on a whole. So truly move on because Ishawna did move on without you.

Let her live to raise your child come on now. Also, you had no right to disrespect that young girl like that. How would you like it if someone disrespected your child and or daughter like that? Yes a grown party (grown people party) was no place for her to be because she was under age from what I gather. But you had no right to belittle her like that. She did not belittle you hence you owe her an apology. But coo pan yu tu. Grow up and get a life because the one you are living is truly not your own. You are living on borrowed time remember that because di next oman yu shame; yu will ha more dan a massive stroke and or heart attack. Retribution is a bitch so truly look into your life because no one is buying your foolishness and bullshit.

Further, what right do you have to want to take her (Ishawna's) life? You are not insane, so let it. You're still holding on to her (Ishawna). So truly don't come with the madhouse and madarks business and bullshit because those that have eyes do see and we do warn. Your child with Ishawna is important, so why do you want to ex her out of life?

Do you not value the life of your child with her?

Why do you want that child to grow mother and fatherless? Come on now.

What you are doing is fucked up fi real.
Thus the games you are playing must stop fi real.

It's not just your life that is important. Ishawna's life is important too.

You Ishawna need to truly grow up and look over your shoulder. I am not threatening you because it seems you don't know what a clock a strike when it comes to you an dis man. Guard your life dummy. Yu di dey a sell good up an nuh noa sey plan a mek anna set fi yu.

You claimed and or said Foota Hype abuse you but yet you truly don't get it.

Do you see your own life before you?
Do you see the life of your child before you?

<u>Do you truly know the mentally and or the mental state of men that abuse women?</u>

I am not saying for you to live on pins and needles but secure your life. This insanity bullshit by Foota is just a ploy and you have to be careful when it comes to this man. A could guh furda but I won't because you truly do not know.

Like I said, **<u>no judge can charge an insane man for insanity. It is ethically and morally wrong because that person was not in their right frame of mind. All they (judges) can do is lock these people in mental institutions away from society.</u>**

So truly be careful in your goings and coming in. You are duly warned because the life you save might be your own.

Once again, Foota it's over. Ishawna moved on and you have to move on too. You caused her harm mentally and physically including sexually because she's like a merry go round for men. You prostituted her out and now she's left your fold; truly leave her alone and let her live; raise the child the both of you have in peace.

You cannot leave your child with her and the other children you have out there crying for a mother and a father come on now. You have to be the bigger man and take responsibility for your own actions as well.

You abused her and she found a way out. If you truly loved and cared for her, you would not have abused and degrade her like that.

No one likes abuse.
Abuse makes people hate you. Just take a look at the abuse our ancestors went through and the hate we as people and or a nation and race have for them including their children.

Think about the abuse many black people are still going through.

Just take a look in Jamaica and see the injustice of our people out there including you. Look at what you did to that young girl, so truly be fair because you do not own Ishawna nor do you control her. She wanted out and she got out. Took the way that was given to her out and I truly do not blame her. You need to grow positively as well as grow up. Look into your life and make wise decisions not just for you but for your children also. Life is worth and she is living her life.

You are living your life so truly live come on now. Stop with your nonsense because your actions are seen and known and you cannot run away from it. So squash it because you did not make Ishawna, she made herself.

She is in control of her own destiny now; so let her live it because you are living yours. You have a new born think of that child also.

You cannot take that child's right to life from them. You are a father, so act as such and be a true father by growing the hell up. It's over get the hell over it and man up. Do your part as a true father and leave Ishawna the hell alone.

__Yes I am coming inside your head because I know your thinking and what you will do to keep you alive whilst making people think you are insane.__

You are not mad just well taught in the art of insanity. No not well taught because I'm in your head. Know what you are thinking. And don't try it with the pills because I know the effect of them. __It's a wicked and evil man premeditates murder and use the insanity plea to get off.__

Yes this is your calm and or plan before the storm, hence Ishawna you need to be careful.

Do not walk alone and if you are going out alone let family members know exactly where you are going.

Your life is important no matter how I bash you. Truly think because **NO ABUSED WOMAN IS SAFE ON THE FACE OF THIS PLANET WHILST THEIR ABUSER STILL WALKS THE EARTH. AND EVEN IN DEATH NO ABUSED WOMAN IS SAFE FROM THEIR ABUSER.** *So truly think and secure yourself from this man.*

Allelujah have mercy Lord because things are not right. Something is truly not right. Allelujah. Wow.

ISHAWNA TRULY BE CAREFUL BECAUSE THE LIFE YOU SAVE IS TRULY YOUR OWN.

As for you Bunny Wailer, let the Rita Marley bullshit go.

HOW THE HELL CAN YOU SAY RITA KILLED BOB MARLEY?

BOB MARLEY KILLED BOB MARLEY PERIOD.

Stop tarnishing this woman's name. Listen, many of us do not like her, but by you saying she murdered Bob is beyond me and my scope of thought, reasoning and sight to blurnaught.

DO YOU HAVE PROOF THAT RITA KILLED BOB?

YOUR HATRED OF RITA IS NOT WARRANTED. SO TRULY STOP YOUR FUCKERY BECAUSE YOU JEALOUSY SUPERSEDES YOU. YOU ARE A PETTY LITTLE MAN THAT HAS NO SOUL OR CONSCIENCE.

Vile and deceitful is what you are thus you have no good light in you or around you. Allelujah. It's not all about you because you are irrelevant; thus you were never a true part of this group.

You knew not the people that you were around thus you truly did not know Bob nor did you truly know Peter.

The head of the Wailers table was not Bob Marley but Peter Tosh.

*Go back to Rastafari Is by Peter Tosh because this song has nothing to do with Haile Selassie **the man you worship.***

*Check the beat that drives your spirit and connects you to a higher force. KNOW THIS; **RASTA'S WERE AROUND LONG BEFORE HAILE SELASSIE. The hair on your head as called lox and or dreadlocks is the hair of the death angels when they walk on the planet earth.** So Rasta's whether you like it or not, you keep the order of death when it comes to your hair. You* *are the death angels. This is how I saw it and this is how I am relating it back to you.*

___Thus all of you worship and praise a dead man that has nothing to do with life but has all to do with Babylon; DEATH.___

Ethiopians are Babylonians because they sold out Lovey (God) long before Adam and Eve. This is partially why BLACKS ARE HATED GLOBALLY. WE KEEP GIVING UP LOVEY BY ACCEPTING ALL THAT WE ARE NOT TO DO. And yes this is also partially why Ethiopia is mentioned in the BOOK OF SIN AND DEATH; YOUR SO CALLED HOLY BIBLE.

LOVEY GAVE JAMAICA HIS NAME, HIS BREATH OF LIFE AND WHAT DO JAMAICANS DO? WE SELL OUT LOVEY EVERY CHANCE WE GET THAN CRY FOUL. So truly take your hatred and bullshit someplace else.

Stop tarnishing this woman's name by talking shit because of YOUR JEALOUSY. Yes you are entitled to your own opinion but your hatred is not warranted period.

__YOU ARE NOT ENTITLED TO ANY OF BOB MARLEY'S MONEY OR ESTATE. HIS KIDS ARE BECAUSE THEY ARE HIS CHILDREN.__ Take your shit and shit talk and go and or continue to burn in hell because you are there already. Thus you are left behind; cannot reside with Bob in the

Valley of the Kings. You do not belong there because of your hatred and pettiness.

TRULY LISTEN TO TIME WILL TELL BECAUSE YOU'RE A FUCKING BALD HEAD THAT SEEKS RELEVANCE BUT CANNOT GET ANY BECAUSE YOUR HEART STINKS AND IS MORE THAN FUCKING CORRUPTED.

HENCE I DEDICATE TIME WILL TELL BY BOB MARLEY TO YOU. You're all fucking petty including the fucking members of the I-THREES.

Let your animosity go because BOB DID MAKE RITA HIS LIFE PARTNER AND CHOICE. He did not make any of you. He made her; so GET THE FUCK OVER IT AND SQUASH THE BC BEEF YOU'RE ALL HARBOURING.

It's amazing after all these years unnu caane live properly; good. Life isn't about petty shit, it's about life. Move on because I know many of you cannot forgive. And it matters not what many of you think, SHE (RITA) WAS CHOSEN SO LEAVE IT AT THAT. Grow the fuck and hell up now man come on now. Some a unnu suh cold inna unnu heart dat hell itself has frozen over with unnu hatred and vileness of hatred in thoughts.

Heal because it's over come on now. And for you Bunny to do this, I truly hope Bob does not forgive you in the grave.

*He Bob had a job to do and he did it because music was what he was given. **He was given Redemption Songs and he told you this. He gave his people the redemption songs given to him but yet his people refused his words; songs.***

NO WONDER ZION FAILED IN THE SPIRITUAL REALM BECAUSE WE AS A PEOPLE REFUSE THE TRUTH WHEN WE ARE GIVEN IT.

*Remember this Bunny. He (Robert Nesta Marley otherwise known as Bob Marley) was crowned King in the spiritual realm and this you cannot take from him because **HE DID HIS JOB. NOT EVEN HAILE SELASSIE CAN SAY THIS. NO KING OR QUEEN THAT IS LIVING OR DEAD CAN SAY THIS, BUT BOB MARLEY CAN. HE SANG BECAUSE THAT WAS WHAT LOVEY GAVE HIM. LOVEY GAVE HIM REDEMPTION SONGS BUT UNNU SUH FUCKING FOOL FOOL DAT UNNU HATE DI MAN AUNDA DI QUIET.** Now you're coming with your bullshit of hate and distrust; misguidance.*

HE WAS CHOSEN AND NOT YOU. IF YOUR HEART WAS CLEAN YOU WOULD HAVE BEEN CHOSEN.

So for you to say Rita killed di man FUCK YOU.

Bob Marley killed himself by doing what he was not supposed to do.

He procreated outside the realms of his marriage to Rita and because of this, he sinned. This is strike one for anyone that is walking with Lovey and disobeys his commandments and or law and laws.

YOU CANNOT GO OUT OF HIS FOLD AND LIVE AN UNCLEAN LIFE NO MATTER HOW TEMPTING THAT LIFE IS. SO FOR YOU TO SAY RITA KILLED HIM THINK.

STRIKE TWO. HE BOB MARLEY INTERFERED IN THE POLITICS OF JAMAICA. HE JOINED SEAGA AND MANLEY TOGETHER AND HE SHOULD HAVE NEVER DONE THIS. WHEN YOU ARE CHOSEN AND WALKING ON THE PATHWAY OF LOVEY; YOU CANNOT INTERFERE IN THE POLITICS OF YOUR COUNTRY OR ANYONE.

YOU CANNOT BREAK THE CODE OF TRUTH AND CLEANLINESS COME ON NOW.

He Bob Marley did this.

Politics is death *and when you interfere in death; you are killed. You are taking death's people away from him and her and you cannot do this if you are not ordained to. You cannot interfere with death because Lovey and or Good God and Allelujah did not tell us to interfere in the politics and churches; whore houses of dead. So truly get your* *facts straight before you open your lying and deceitful mouth.*

STRIKE THREE. He went to Germany to get medical aide thus he was killed and or died in Germany. WHEN YOU BECOME A THREAT TO DEATH, DEATH HAS THE RIGHT AND CAN TAKE YOU BY ANY MEANS NECESSARY. You interfered in the course of death by going into Death's domain. Religion and politics belong to death and Bob interfered in both. He accepted death because he did accept a Babylonian King as his God and you cannot do this if you are chosen by Lovey. _Certain lands you cannot go into also because these lands are not the domain of life. You cannot go against life if you are with life and chosen by life come on now._ Thus the things Lovey has and have forbidden you to do, you cannot do. I've shown and told you this in some of my other books. Know that many diseases are created in laboratories around the globe and Cancer is no exception. Therefore, they said he Bob had Toe Cancer. Thus death killed and or took Bob from the living. Figure it out because Cancer is the 4th sign of the Zodiac that falls in the 6th month of the calendar year. Thus your 4

and 20 elders which is the 24000 years Satan and his people have; well had to deceive humanity and take them to hell. Put it together if you can. No you can't because I just did it for you. And this is if you are going by the bullshit calendar that we are given. There is truly 13 months plus a day in the true human calendar. But because 13 is loathed by some; 13 was changed to represent 12; half the cycle of death. And yes I know 4 represent Aries the God of war. So every fourth cycle death must come for some due to sacrifice.

The proper human calendar should be:

M 1	M 2	M 3	M 4	M 5	M 6	M 7	M 8	M 9	M 10	M 11	M 12	M 13
28	28	28	28	28	28	28	28	28	28	28	28	29

M represents months

Thus the code is:

JAN	FEB	MAR	APR	MAY	JUN	JUL	AUG	SEP	OCT	NOV	DEC
3	0	3	2	3	2	3	3	2	3	2	3

Which give you 29 days in the final month; month 13.
Therefore, people fear 13 thus fearing death and I truly do not know why. You cannot fear death if you have true life.

So you cannot say you are doing the work of Lovey and walk with death under the quiet. Death will take you and this is what has and have happened to him. Thus he's *resting the Valley of the Kings with his ancestors before him. Those who walk on both paths; LIFE AND DEATH.*

So for you to be so petty just tells me you are jealous of this woman and will forever be jealous of her. In my book you are a demon because you are willing to taint someone's image due to jealousy and hate. And none of you better look at me when it comes to these books. What I see and know and what is given to me is what I share and or give to you.

NO WONDER JAMAICA AND THE RASTA COMMUNITY CANNOT BE BETTER. UNNU CHAT BOUT UNITY AN NOT ONE A UNNU HA UNITY IN UNNU HEART. THUS NONE OF YOU KNOW THE LIFE LOVEY, GOOD GOD AND ALLELUJAH HAS AND HAVE GIVEN TO JAMAICA.

Like I said, listen to Rastafari Is by Peter Tosh and get a fucking clue. You all worship a fucking man that was a BC Babylonian by decent and not one of you can see this. Try going on the internet if they have not taken this down and listen to Selassie generation tell you that they can trace their lineage through to Nimrod and all the way into Babylon (India) in the time of old. So fuck all of you that SAY BUN BABYLON BUT YET PRAISE AND WORSHIP BABYLON GODS – MAN; MEN. And to be truly honest with you I truly don't care if RASTAS GLOBALLY HATE ME BECAUSE NONE OF YOU KNOW AMBUSH IN THE NIGHT.

BOB WAS TRYING TO EDUCATE YOU FOOL FOOL LOTS OF IGNORANT APATHETIC FOOLS AND NONE OF YOU COULD AND OR CAN FIGURE IT OUT.

Truly thank you to the coordinator of Rootz Reggae Radio for this new word. Each one teach one.

Shout out to Rootz Reggae Radio for having me on their program September 29, 2015. I truly enjoyed myself and we must do this again. You gave me my first shot at life when it came to promoting my books and I will never forget this.

Thank you Wylie the Barber on Eglinton (Eglinton and Times Road near Eglinton and Oakwood) for introducing me to Mr. Courtney Blackstar. You gave me an opening and I did take it and truly loved it.

So Mr. Blackstar, truly thank you for the opening and opportunity you gave me.

And to all the Rastas' globally; think because YOU'RE ALL A BUNCH OF PAGAN HYPOCRITES THAT PRAISE AND WORSHIP BABYLON. UNNU TELL LIES THUS UNNU SPREAD LIES; THE LIES OF BABYLON INNA UNNU MUSIC.

Guh fi di bible because nuff a unnu use it. DID NOT THE BIBLE SAY ISRAEL IS AND OR WAS DESTROYED; WAS NO

MORE. SO IF ISRAEL IS NO MORE, WHY ARE YOU FOLLOWING ETHIOPIA; ISRAEL?

FOOL FOOL BLACK PEOPLE, WEY CLASSICALLY CONDITIONED UNDER THE RELIGIOUS BULLSHIT OF LIIES THAT YOU'VE BEEN FED; WAKE THE FUCK UP AND KNOW YOUR TRUE HISTORY; TRUTH.

STOP SPREADING LIES ON YOUR OWN LINEAGE DUMMY.

You in Jamaica, Lovey gave you his name JAMAICA WHICH STANDS FOR AND OR MEAN GOD (JA) MADE ME.

He gave you his flag WHICH IS THE TRUE FLAG OF LIFE AND NUFF A UNNU DEAD; DREADFUL BEASTS PUT THE FLAG OF LIFE DOWN ANNA WAVE DI ETHIOPIAN FLAG LIKE ALL BLACK PEOPLE COME FROM AFRICA.

ALL BLACK PEOPLE DID NOT COME FROM AFRICA.

BLACKS COULD BE FOUND IN CHINA, ICELAND, EVERYWHERE ON THE FACE OF THIS PLANET BECAUSE IT WAS A BLACK GOD THAT CREATED IT ALL AND THIS HAS NOTHING TO DO WITH COLOUR OF SKIN; HUE. No one can take this from us because the truth is in us.

THE FOUNDATION OF LIFE IS BLACK. SO OUT OF THE DARKNESS WE CAME AND INTO THE LIGHT WE GROW DUMMIES. Yes I am mad for what this man said and I will not apologize for calling any of unnu fool fool and dummy including dummies.

Marcus Mosiah Garvey did tell us. A people without knowledge of their history are like trees without roots. And I will not stop telling you this. Blacks had to be colonized and raped of their history, roots and dignity; life. We were left for dead and we are partially to blame for this, but yet none can see and or acknowledge the sins of our forefathers including us in this day and time. **_We have to stop blaming and start cleaning if we want to survive this brutal harvest that's coming._**

Lovey also gave us his breath of life Y(ALLAH)S; ALLAH. TAKE THE Y AND S OFF AND YOU GET ALLAH. ALLAH STANDS FOR AND OR MEAN THE BREATH OF LIFE, **_BUT THOSE DECEITFUL BABYLONIANS THAT CONTAMINATED THIS WAY OF LIFE CLAIMS THEY HAVE IT WHEN THEY DO NOT. JAMAICAN HAVE IT BUT YET DESTROYED IT WITH UNNU GUN MAN FOOLISHNESS AND KILLING FOOLISHNESS._**

Eediats of people globally, **_EVERY BLACK LAND WAS TO FALL. IF DI DEBIL COULD NOT GET INTO LOVEY'S KINGDOM HE WAS GOING TO MAKE SURE HIS CHILDREN_**

DID NOT GET IN ALSO. LIKE OLE PEOPLE SEY, IF YU CAANE GET QUAKOO YU MUSS GET SHUT. AND THIS IS WHAT THE DEVIL AND HIS PEOPLE DID TO THE BLACK RACE.

Thus the devil could not get to Lovey; Good God and Allelujah, but he sure as hell got to his children and look at the black race (not based on hue) globally.

Wi cum eene like dem staving dawg dem wey a beg bone to rass.

We've become so conditioned in our thinking and thought process that we're lost to rass.

Coo pan di shit we as a people believe in. Dem gi wi wi owna watered down history that has been falsified and wi believe it.

Dem tell wi sey in order for us to live we have to accept death. Accept death mi rass. When mi dead mi dead. Mi nuh ha life, so wey mi a accept death fa?

Mi waane live. Mi nuh waane dead like yu.

Think. Life is your right not death come on now.
Yu waane dead so dead, but don't take me with you.

Like I've said to Lovey, I truly do not care if every race on the face of this planet hates me. Life is worth living and if they want to die for death so be it. Let them fucking die because you cannot be telling people to choose life and they continuously choose death. An wen dem dead dem a guh sey a fi yu fault; you did not secure them.

We knew the lies of death because death people told you what they were going to do to you; they have to it's the law. DEATH TOLD YOU YOU SHOULD NOT FOLLOW HIM but instead of listening to the commandments of Death; well Life, humans follow death blindly to their deaths.

Wi come in like di blind mice dem and di foolish women dem of old that did not put oil in their lamps. In our case today, we do not clean our selves nor do we put cleanliness first; in our life and lamp; good store houses.

I truly don't care if the black race hates me because I am truly sick of the lots of them. ***Lovey cannot be giving you ALL THE FUCKING TRUTH FOR CENTURIES AND YOU KEEP REJECTING HIM FOR BULLSHIT.***

SATAN DON'T LIKE NONE OF YA'LL. YOU'RE ALL HIS BITCH THAT HE HANDS OVER TO DEATH; SO WAKE THE FUCK UP AND DO FUCKING BETTER AS A FUCKING RACE AND PEOPLE. *STOP SICK MI TUMMUCK WITH UNNU BULLSHIT. TU FUCKING PAC TOLD YOU IN CHANGES AND STILL AS A RACE AND PEOPLE WE REFUSE TO LEARN. SUH TEK UNNU BEATING.*

Stop fucking complaining and live with the shit unnu a get because unnu tek up every shit of another man's race and culture an sey a fi unnu.

Wey fi unnu dey:
Wey eee dey?

If you had known the truth, would you not know the full truth of you and your life story from the past to the present?

So don't tell me shit because like I said, the truth is in us and as Bob said, if you listen carefully you will hear. Natural Mystic

The woman of Zion, BLACK RACE LOST IN 2015 AND NOW THE MONGOLIANS AND OR CHINESE IS POISED TO TAKE CONTROL AND THERE IS NOTHING THAT ANY OF YOU CAN DO TO CHANGE THIS.

THEY ACCEPTED THE YING AND YANG BECAUSE MOSES GAVE IT TO THEM AND THEY KEPT TRUE TO THE YING AND YANG UNTIL THIS DAY. NOW TELL ME WHAT THE FUCK DOES THE BLACK RACE HAVE? WE KEEP REJECTING INSTEAD OF TRULY KNOWING. RELIGION IS DEATH.

AMERICA GOT THE UPWARD EYE IN TRIANGLE AND WHAT DO THEY DO, MOCK THE FUCK OUT OF THE

TRIANGLE WHILST RACKING UP A DEBT IN THE TRILLIONS FOR DEATH. AND WHEN MARCUS GARVEY WENT TO THEM TO SAY WAIT A MINUTE YOU CANNOT DO THIS, RACK UP SO MUCH DEBT THEY TARNISHED THE MAN'S IMAGAE. NOW LOOK AT AMERICA.

People strung out on drugs and millions homeless in the streets.

Why?

Was it all called for?

Look at your fucking penitentiaries; overloaded with young black males and females whilst the government have some of their children living in the crack houses of pedophiles, pedophiles that use and abuse them sexually, mentally and spiritually.

So yes we are fucked up and jacked up as a race. Thus WE DO NOT KNOW OUR TRUE ROOTS. **OUR TREE OF LIFE IS FUCKING DEAD IN A SYSTEM THAT WAS DESIGNED TO KEEP THE RICH RICHER AND THE POOR POORER.**

So truly fuck all of ya'll because we as a nation of people truly do not listen. All some a wi du a maggle and pap style like wi a sumady.

Many a unnu talk bout unnu care but when it comes down to it none a wi fucking care.

Money too good thus many a unnu sell unnu soul fi money.

Many a unnu name inna death's book and it's a matter of time before people si unnu true colours.

Bunch a fucking hypocrites that sell death inna unnu music and video dem. We as black people are the ones selling death to our people. So tell me, how the hell do you care; if you are giving your own death to live by?

None a unnu clean, hence it's only a matter of time before all a unnu come tumbling down.

Di sea calm now but ooh what a la la when the sea comes to life; roar and tumble down; destroy.

KNOW YOUR FUCKING TRUE HISTORY. BOB MARLEY TOLD YOU HOW. LISTEN TO NATURAL MYSTIC BECAUSE THE TRUTH IS ENGRAINED IN US. THE TRUTH CANNOT BE ERODED FROM OUR DNA BECAUSE THE SPIRIT IS OUR TRUE LIFE. IT (THE SPIRIT) IS OUR PATHWAY TO LIFE AND DEATH. SO PICK YOUR CHOICE.

Going back to repatriation and how Jamaica wants 25 billion dollars from England and or the European nations for slavery.

WOW MI MUMMA TO YASS.
Really Jamaica?

ARE YOU THAT FUCKING STUPID?

AS FOR UNNU SO CALLED HISTORIANS THAT ARE TALKING, UNNU PATHETIC. UNNU DID GET UNNU DEGREE IN STUPIDITY?

You're all a bunch of fucking jokes that need to be black listed from the black community indefinitely. Thus I did not listen to unnu words because it's the same old same old where black people looking for a financial handout from the European community.

BUT EUROPE FOOL FOOL DOA.

IF I WAS THE EUROPEAN UNION I WOULD LAUGH ALL A UNNU BLACK IDIOTS TO SCORN.

MORONS IN JAMAICA BLACK PEOPLE SOLD BLACK PEOPLE AS SLAVES. CHECK UNNU SELF. NO UNNU CAANE CHECK UNNU SELF BECAUSE ALL A UNNU A FUCKING WRECKING BALL TO RAWTID.

YOU CANNOT IN GOOD FAITH SEEK REPATRIATION FROM THE EUROPEAN NATIONS ALONE. AFRICA, YES MAMA AFRICA MUST PAY YOU REPATRIATION ALSO BECAUSE THEY; OUR ANCESTORS OF OLD, FUCKING SOLD US TO THE HIGHEST BIDDER. THEY TRAFFICKED US; WERE INVOLVED IN HUMAN TRAFFICKING AND OR SLAVERY LONG BEFORE THE EUROPEANS CAME ALONG. So you can't look to one country to be paid a handout, you have to look to all globally. India must pay you too because they were the first to start with the enslavement bullshit. Read your fucking bibles and know the truth.

Go back to Egypt.

Go further back to Ethiopia before Adam and Eve if you can.

We sold our own out. So why the fuck should EUROPEANS PAY US AND NOT AFRICA ALSO?

WE WANT AN APOLOGY, THEN AFRICA SHOULD APOLOGIZE TO US AS A PEOPLE, RACE AND NATION BECAUSE THEY DID SELL US; THEY DID DO THEIR OWN PEOPLE WRONG.

WHY SHOULD ALL OTHER NATIONS APOLOGIZE AND NOT THEM? I'm not a fucking hypocrite because I KNOW FOR A FACT THAT THE DEVIL CANNOT COME INTO YOUR LAND UNLESS YOU LET HIM IN. GO BACK TO EVE (HAWWAH).

She let the devil into her household, kingdom and she got cast the hell out of Lovey's world and domain. She could never get back into Lovey's abode because she went against Lovey. She disobeyed him and went with death. So as a race, don't tell me shit because the truth is embedded in some of the lies you read.

Go there with it an mek mi cuss out unnu claate.

Wake the fuck up and know your dirty ancestral history and or past.

We sold our own to the Babylonians and we did enslave our own. GO BACK TO NIMROD'S DIRTY PAST WITH HIS FUCKING BULLSHIT. No wonder some a unnu hole true to Islam. Lovey took us out of it because Babylon polluted it and look dey, wi still inna it anna kill wi people dem fi it.

WE CANNOT GO BACK INTO A LAND OR CULTURE THAT LOVEY CONDEMNS. WE HAVE TO STAY THE HELL OUT. *Yes it's hard but we have to try no matter the cost. Come on now.*

Unnu a begga?

Fucking apologize to self and LET FUCKING AFRICA APOLOGIZE FOR THEIR BULLSHIT ALSO. Africa did her people wrong. Thus Africa must take some of the blame also.

YOU CANNOT LOOK FOR MONETARY COMPENSATION FROM ONE LAND AND NOT THE OTHER BECAUSE AFRICA DID SELL US. WE DID SELL EACH OTHER, BUT AS BLACK WE FAIL TO ADMIT OUR DIRTY AND NASTY PAST.

Fuck all of you. I need no apologies from Europe. I need it from Africa, our so called fucking black own.

What the hell makes Africa so fucking righteous that they cannot apologize?

THEY WERE THE ONES TO LET THE FUCKING DEVIL IN AND LOOK AT THE WORLD GLOBALLY TODAY.

WE CAUSED THE FUCKING MESS AND IT'S US AS A RACE AND PEOPLE THAT MUST FIX IT.

OTHER'S CANNOT FIX OUR PROBLEMS. WE KNOW THEM SO FUCKING FIX THEM BY START APOLOGIZING TO LOVEY FOR CONSTANTLY CHOOSING EVIL AND THE BULLSHIT OF EVIL OVER HIM. WE SAY GOD AND GOOD OVER EVIL, BUT NOT ONE OF US A PART FROM ME HAVE AND HAS TOLD LOVEY SORRY FOR WHAT OUR ANCESTORS DID TO HIM AND US AS A PEOPLE.

Pick the fucking beam out of our eyes first before we can pick it out of someone else's come on now. We rape each other as a people then cry foul.

We keep each other down instead of building each other positively.

WE HAVE NOT DONE RIGHT FOR SELF AS A PEOPLE BUT YET WE WANT OTHERS TO DO RIGHT BY US.

Well fuck you.

Get a fucking life and clue.

THE BLACK RACE DID NOT JUST COME ABOUT LIKE THAT. BUT THEN AGAIN, I SHOULD NOT BE MAD BECAUSE NOT ALL BLACKS ARE OF GOD; GOOD GOD AND ALLELUJAH; LOVEY.

So Jamaica get off your fucking pump and pride and kiss it. No one owes you nothing. Bunch a fucking morons that can't run di country right. You keep your people enslaved and poor whilst you as a government misrepresent, misguide, abuse, refuse; murder and kill.

WHY THE FUCK DON'T THE CITIZENS OF THE LAND CHARGE ALL OF YOU INEPT GOVERNMENT OFFICIALS $25

BILLION EUROS FOR MISMANAGEMENT AND DECEIVING THE PEOPLE OF JAMAICA AND THE WORLD?

As government officials unnu value di life a di people dem?

Unnu nuh leave dem in want?

Unnu nuh rob the country of its finances and resources. Now unnu want sumady else; the EUROPEAN NATIONS TO PAY FI UNNU FUCKRY.

Buoy duppy truly noa who fi frighten to rass.

White people; well Europeans the middle finger and hand is there. You are authorized to give every Jamaican in Jamaica and abroad the middle finger and stamp stupidity on their heads.

Jamaica is broke and the $25 billion they are asking for truss mi will not go towards paying off the national debt of the land. Di money a guh line dem packet.

This was well thought out, hence Portia's husban mi rate yu. Yu thief nuh rass eeene. Wow.

Smile because we know Portia is not smarten than a fifth grader because she did not go to university. She's the only uneducated dunce to run a country. But then she's not running it. You an Patterson a run di country under the quiet.

Maybe when she grows some balls and start treating the people of the land with respect and dignity I will begin to like her. NOT.

Jamaicans and Jamaica deserves better so do fucking better.

Remember JamaicaF. Thus Jamaica did fail God; Lovey and you're all living on borrowed time. Thus the sea is calm right now, but when she explodes; trust me, Jamaica will be destroyed because unnu sell out every damned thing Lovey gave unto you. Thus black people are SO NOT FUCKING LOYAL TO LOVEY. THEY ARE ONLY LOYAL TO DEATH. AS A NATION AND PEOPLE THEY GIVE DEATH EVERYTHING AND DEN CRY TO LOVEY. Some a unnu not even respect the Jamaican flag.

All a unnu Rastas pose up the Ethiopian flag like all Black people come from Ethiopia.

Some a unnu bout di Ethiopian flag take precedence over the Jamaican flag.

Well a hope when destruction comes to di land of Jamaica unnu sey Selassie High save me because I know for a fact Lovey will not save the lots of you. Unnu put Babylon first *and mek him Lovey (Jah), his name and flag lost. If that makes any sense. In a nut shell, unnu tun di name an flag of Lovey into a joke. Unnu bun Babylon but yet praise and worship Babylon to repeat myself.*

When unnu a dead fi hungry mi hope Selassie can bring unnu food and wata including gi unnu shelta.

Yes I've created enemies in all of you so truly think. IF LOVEY DID NOT TRULY LOVE YOUR LAND HE WOULD NOT HAVE GIVEN YOU HIS NAME, HIS FLAG AND HIS BREATH OF LIFE.

THE TRUTH DOES NOT RESIDE IN AFRICA. IT RESIDES IN JAMAICA BECAUSE THIS IS THE LAND WHERE EVERY FACET OF TRUTH IS COMING OUT OF. YOU AS THE PEOPLE OF THE LAND ARE THE ONES TO DESTROY THE TRUTH INCLUDING SELF. WAVE THE FLAG OF LIFE, JAMAICA BECAUSE THIS IS THE ONLY FLAG THAT CAN SAVE US ALL; YOU.

YES THERE ARE SPIRITUAL FLAGS BUT WE MUST FIRST ACCEPT AND RESPECT OUR OWN BEFORE WE CAN TRULY BRING PEACE TO THE WORLD. BE PROUD OF YOUR TRUE JAMAICAN OWN MAN COME ON NOW.

Reclaim your true heritage by starting to wave the Jamaican Flag. Show Lovey that you are truly proud of this flag come on now. Show him Lovey that you truly want and need him in your good up good up life.

Why the hell should we pose up Israel when LOVEY MADE US HIS OWN TRUE PEOPLE AND CREATION?

Learn the truth and know the truth.

Stop killing the truth.

Make the changes in you because LOVEY DID NOT TELL ME HE WANTED HIS HOME IN AFRICA. HE WANTS IT IN THE CAYMAN ISLANDS; the Caribbean.

LOVEY'S HOME SHOULD HAVE BEEN BUILT IN JAMAICA, BUT WE AS A NATION AND PEOPLE HAVE PROVEN TO HIM LOVEY THAT WE WOULD RATHER LIVE DIRTY AND DO ALL THAT IS DIRTY AND FILTHY BEFORE WE ACCEPT HIM AND LIVE BY THE TRUTH.

COO DEY
COO DEY

ANOTHER NATION TOOK PRECEDENCE OVER THE LOTS OF YOU. YOU'VE MADE JAMAICA SO FUCKING DIRTY THAT LOVEY HAS AND HAVE DEEMED THE ISLAND UNCLEAN. WE DID THIS PEOPLE, NO ONE ELSE BUT US DID THIS. So when hard times come, truly do not blame Lovey, blame self because hard times is coming; thus death must and will get his pay.

It's so shameful that all we asked for Lovey gave to us and we could not abide by our word.

Don't look at me because despite me telling Lovey I am leaving him, I am still with him.

So now if we cannot love Lovey true; how the hell do we expect him to love us true?

How the hell do we expect him to help us when we can't even help him or honour our words?

Thus repatriation and Zion is dead.

And people and family; my true family, I make no apologies for the contents in this book. I had to get things off my chest and I did; thus the hot and spiciness of this book. The truth needed to be told in a harsh way.

We cannot expect Lovey to save us when we are not doing anything to save ourselves.

We can't keep robbing each other and selling out each other and think it is sitting well with God; Good God and Allelujah; Lovey come on now.

HOW THE HELL CAN WE SING IT IS WELL WHEN ALL IS NOT WELL IN EARTH AND IN OUR SOUL; SPIRIT?

The lies have to stop.

We know the churches of the globe feed and sell you death; hell and all that is sinful.

We know the politicians of the globe buy death because they take your hard earned tax money and buy arms. They rob you of your decent future, but yet none of us can see this. ***So tell me, HOW CAN GOD; LOVEY SAVE US IF WE CONSTANTLY BUY DEATH?***

Michelle Jean

Unnu noa sey mi nuh hole back nothing when it comes to these books.

I go hard and speak my mind come what may.

We cannot talk the talk and do not walk the good walk come on now.

I am truly fed up of us as a people wining and pining about slavery. Get the fuck over it and do something to change the lies that was told about our ancestors.

I was not born from a fucking slave nor was my ancestors' slaves or indentured servants. **I WILL NOT TEACH MY CHILDREN THIS; NOR WILL I LET THEM BRAND THEMSELVES AS CHILDREN OF SLAVES.**

We as black people have a nasty past and if you want to be branded as slaves and the weak; by all means go the fuck ahead. I know the creators and inventors we were.

We took things too far because we did sell our own people.

We did let the devil and his children into our world and realm. **I will not take away from that, but do not label me a slave and or descendants of slaves when I was not. Do not tell me all BLACK PEOPLE ORIGINATED FROM AFRICA WHEN ALL BLACK PEOPLE DID NOT ORIGINATE FROM AFRICA. MANY BLACK ARE OF EUROPEAN LINEAGE BY**

DESCENT AND BIRTH FROM WAY BEFORE THE DAYS OF OLD AND OR THAT WHICH WAS TOLD TO YOU BY LIARS.

We were originally in Europe and or Eurasian lands long before the white people as we call them came along.

Thus we were told by Marcus Mosiah Garvey, a people without knowledge of their history are like trees without roots. Which means we are dead, and we are dead THUS REVELATIONS CALL US THE FIRST BEGOTTEN OF THE DEAD.

As a race and nation we have no true roots because we've been colonized; colonized to the point where we do not have a true language for ourselves.

We know not our true history and or life stories; truths.

We have no customs of our own.

We've lost our beauty and cleanliness.

We've been raped and abused and left for dead.

We've become devalued and valueless in the societies of men.

We're jailed and are used as jail bait.

THUS WE WILL FOREVER BE SHACKLED AND CHAINED IN OUR OWN IGNORANCE, LIES AND DECEIT.

We are taught wrong, thus we educate our own wrong. And when the truth comes along you all kill the truth because the truth does not justify your lying and deceiving ways.

And none of you can say I am wrong because the lady that wanted to and did start the Afro centric School at Keele and Sheppard comes to mind.

WI FIGHT DI OMAN DUNG SUH TILL SHE STRESS OUT.

We say we want better for self and community AND WHEN BETTER COMES, WE FIGHT DOWN THE BETTER.

We say we need a system for our self, but yet destroy those that want to give you a better system and a better way.

SO HOW THE FUCK CAN WE HAVE A BETTER WAY WHEN WE KEEP TRAPPING OURSELVES IN HELL?

We sit on our asses and expect someone to come and hold our hands and take us out of the mess and messes we've put ourselves in.

We live a bullshit life and teach our children the same bullshit. So how the hell can we be better and do better? Bullshit nuh beget bullshit. Thus we have bullshit children that follow on and in the same pathway as their parents.

Thus we are taught lies and we intern teach our children these lies, and when they come and do what we tell them to do; we scold them.

How the hell can we scold our children for lies when we are the ones to teach them to lie and or these lies?

Lies beget lies and people some do steal come on now.

We have to face reality come on now.

I am so sorry but I thought I would include fillers but I've reached my target; so I cannot add fillers to this book.

So as a nation and people we have to think and do better for self.

We have to teach our children better.

And for those of you who say we do not stress each other out. Find the Gully Bop video and si how di people dem inna fi im home town stressed him out to the point where he was left broke and or near broke when he went back there. Some a wi ha family wey live pan wi a farin. Every minute dem hungry like a dem did help you get to farin.

Some a dem want dis, dem want dat like yu a pick money affa tree.

So don't sey mi lie because mi noa wey mi a talk bout.

Suh if yu like mi, falla mi pan twitter. I truly do not tweet alot. But wey mi a ask yu fi falla mi pan twitter fa? I am not a social media junkie. I am just there on twitter and I truly don't know why now.

Mi retweet tweets and hardly tweet things for myself when I am on there. (MichelleJean77 is my twitter account). Noa sey if yu rude, yu a guh get back rudeness. If you cuss mi, mi a guh cuss yu back. If yu threaten mi, I am going to tell you what you can do with those threats.

Yes I am truly not a social media person.

No I am so not on Instagram and I truly do not have Face Book and not going to get them.

It's October 05, 2015 and confusion is all around me in my dream world. Something is so not right because more destruction cometh. I can't remember if I was on another planet and war and or fighting broke out. Therefore, I *cannot tell you if there is going to be another mass killing somewhere.*

I know I dreamt I went to the United States and was preaching and or talking to this white man dressed in black. I am pretty sure he was white. Yes he was white and not black. In the dream I had power; meaning I could go into the land without becoming dirty. See Lovey did not tell me the land itself is dirty. I know the United States is dirty because Sin and or Death own this land. Every vileness of sin and wickedness comes out of this land. Thus when Sin and or Death talk about sin they talk about the United States of America and I've told you this in other books.

NO SIN OF VILENESS AND WICKEDNESS IS OFF LIMIT TO THIS LAND. YOU NAME THE SIN; THE PEOPLE OF THIS LAND DO IT. THUS LIKE JAMAICA, AMERICA; THE UNITED STATES OF AMERICA HAS BECOME THE MODERN DAY SODOM AND JAMAICA IS THE MODERN DAY GOMORRAH; thus Sodom and Gomorrah in this day and time.

So because of vileness of evil and wickedness and yes condemnation (men and women changing sex and the courts of justice giving these people legal rights to lie to humanity about their sex and or gender) condemnation is upon this land.

So every sin of man that you can think of and then some the people in this land do.

Every commandment of God; Good God and Allelujah; Lovey the people in this land break each and every day.

But this book is truly not about America. Yes I've been dreaming about LA and somehow I am missing destruction somewhere. Florida I know is on the targeted list of death but when full destruction comes is another story. As for California I truly don't know if the land itself is going to collapse into the earth; sea but Nevada wow. You too are on the target list of death for destruction and it's a matter of when destruction happens. Thus my dream with the Rock, (Dwayne Johnson and his cousin that use to be in the Shield in the WWE), Busta Rhymes (who took my car in the dream), my son, this white lady that was helpful, animals fighting, cars, houses, a shopping mall and the earth and or ground further collapsing (there was a collapsed hole; huge one there before the earth and or ground collapsed again. This dream is really weird and long so I am going to leave it alone because it does not have to mean California is going to collapse; it could be Samoa. Maybe somewhere in Samoa the earth is going to give way. Like I said, it's a weird dream and this is a dream inna dream thus they are truly hard to figure out. This one is complex and I won't burst my head and or brain over it trying to figure it out.

Yes I am dreaming about water again therefore I told you, there is calm in the seas and I am wondering if this is the calm before the storm. Something is truly wrong but I cannot tell you the wrongs. They are being kept from me and I truly do not know why. Usually death is bare faced and bold. They show me what they are going to do but things have and has changed with the seas on so many levels.

I truly have to wonder if all of Oceania is going to sink.

Something is truly not right in the South Pacific and I cannot tell you what it is because I am kept from seeing it. I know something is wrong there, but Guam I truly do not want to go.

<u>Its early morning and I cannot sleep because I dreamt the destruction of Jamaica again and I woke up out of my sleep.</u> *Could I get back to sleep? No, but I managed to go back. Listen people, I've been dreaming about the destruction of Jamaica for years now and this destruction cannot happen. So I am so not going to concern myself with the destruction of this land. Mi feel it inna mi belly with this dream, but I am so not going to worry because Death has been pissing me off when it comes to the destruction of this land.*

I keep seeing this destruction like I've said, but yet, destruction does not come. So now I ask you Death, what kind of destruction is going to come to Jamaica?

Is the island going to sink or is it destructive political unrest that is going to face the island?

Truly stop taunting me with this land. I know lands are going to sink to the bottom of the sea, but stop lying to me with the destruction of Jamaica bullshit. Was not Japan and Jamaica to be destroyed according to the white man?

So do your job. Who am I to interfere with you?

Now world, I am so tired of repatriation that I so don't want to hear about it. I so don't want to hear discussions on it because repatriation is bullshit.

BLACK PEOPLE WAKE THE FUCK UP AND KNOW THAT WHEN YOU LEAVE LOVEY; GOOD GOD AND ALLELUJAH; GOD AS SOME OF YOU AND ME AT TIMES CALL HIM, SLAVERY IS WHAT YOU FUCKING GET. HE LOVEY LEAVES YOUR ASS ALONE TO BE BRUTALIZED AND KILLED.

ONCE YOU LEAVE HIM FOR DEATH, DEATH IS WHAT YOU FUCKING GET. SO WAKE THE FUCK UP AND LEARN.

Lovey did not cause slavery upon us, we caused it on self. So if you want the brutality to stop, then DO DI RIGHT THING. Elephant Man

Our ancestors let Lovey go long before Adam and Eve. Those lying Ethiopians let the devil into their domain, thus disrespecting Lovey. This is why your bible tells you Israel is no more. THEY LOST THEIR PLACE WITH GOD; LOVEY AND GOD; LOVEY HAS AND STILL HAVE A BONE TO PICK WITH THEM UNTIL THIS DAY.

We know the truth but as a NATION AND PEOPLE WE ACCEPT THE BULLSHIT OF LIES THEY TELL US. **Truly listen to AMBUSH IN THE NIGHT by Bob Marley because he was educating you in this song.**

THUS MARCUS MOSIAH GARVEY SAID, A PEOPLE WITHOUT KNOWLEDGE OF THEIR HISTORY ARE LIKE TREES WITHOUT ROOTS. MEANING WE ARE DEAD AND WE ARE DEAD BECAUSE REVELATIONS CALLED US THE FIRST BEGOTTEN OF THE DEAD.

So wake the fuck up and know your true roots; history.

As for you England and your fucking Bullshit Prime Minister. Obama made history so now you Cameron want to make history as well.

What does Jamaica look like to you?

YOU CAMERON COULD CARE LESS ABOUT JAMAICA.
Don't dodge the bullet when it comes to Jamaica. Your visit was a fucking waste of time and disgrace. Your entire

Caribbean visit is a front and a waste of British tax payers money. England can no longer use the Caribbean. No wait you still do because Black People and Black Lands won't wake up and smell the deceit that you politicians bring them.

$25 million to build a prison in Jamaica!!

KEEP YOUR DAMNED BLOOD MONEY. WHEN GILBERT AND IVAN AND OTHER HURRICANES DID MASH UP JAMAICA WHERE WAS BRITISH AIDE (MONEY) TO HELP THE LAND AND PEOPLE?

Wi look like poopponennay tu yu?

NOW 2015 A WINE DUNG AN ENGLAND HA MONEY FI THROW AROUND.

Please go someplace else with your bullshit and pittance of not even scrub and dog change. You're a fucking disgrace to humanity with the bullshit you Cameron and Obama is doing. Both of you waving the WHITE FLAG OF DEATH whist expecting people to buy into your demonic bullshit.

60 years of sanctions on Cuba.
Oppression of another man's country and people.

60 years of lies because Cuba won't come your way. So you do all to repress the country and people and take away their right and dignity to live and make a living. All this shit you and England do to other countries and now that DEATH IS GOING TO WALK ON LAND ON A MASSIVE SCALE UNNU A WAVE FLAG LIKE SEY UNNU ACTIONS GOING TO HELP UNNU COUNTRY AND NATION.

America is slated to fall AND SATAN DID TRANSFER HIS POWER TO A HUMAN BEING IN 2013; THUS ENGLAND IS GOING TO GO DOWN AS WELL.

ENGLAND MUST GO DOWN BECAUSE REVELATIONS MUST BE FULFILLED. THE THRONE OF ENGLAND BELONGS TO HIM. THE ONE THAT SATAN TRANSFERRED HIS POWER TO. So truly stop because everything must come to a head and a foot by the end of 2015 if not early 2016.

So Cameron you are not fooling anyone with your shame and bullshit money. Black People are not fools, SO TRULY STOP EMBARRASSING US WITH YOUR RACIST AND FAKE ASS BULLSHIT. It's over globally for humanity.

Satan has possession of many of your lands and the land and people are going to suffer because God as you call him is truly not going to save any of you. No matter how you go to church and or your mosques and or synagogues, Lovey is truly not going to save ya'll because he truly knows you not. Many of you say you are this and that, but yet walk and deceive humans, spread propaganda, cause lands to be raped and robbed of their riches, thus leaving them barren and poor while your country flourish off the backs of these people. All this Lovey sees and knows, thus many White Lands are going to go down to hell and suffer financially, spiritually, emotionally, food and health wise because the water and food of your land (s) must be taken from the lots of you.

Hundreds of Millions; Billions are going to starve because of the wickedness your country and ancestors have and has done to others including their own.

REMEMBER THE DEBTS OF SLAVERY CANNOT BE REPAID BECAUSE MANY BLACK PEOPLE DID CRY AND THEIR TEARS DID FALL ON YOUR LAND AND PEOPLE. THERE PRAYERS IS GOING TO BE ANSWERED THUS I HAVE NO USE FOR REPATRIATION BECAUSE HELL IS THERE FOR EVERY WICKED HUMAN. SO NO APOLOGIES IS NEED BY ME FROM THE WHITE RACE BECAUSE I TRULY KNOW HELL IS THE HOME OF YOU ALL. Well the majority of you anyway. Thus October 6th I dreamt this skinny White Woman. She was alive but she was dead. She worked in a mortuary and or dead house and or funeral home for some. Her petite size is like the picture I used in MY TALK BOOK FOURTEEN – MY TALK WITH GOD, but without the soggy skin. She told me they would not let her in. This lady that I did not see in the dream but can't get the picture of her outside my head would not let her in. I was watching this black model of *average to large size modelling this green dress. Her size and frame is in my head of how the woman in the dream looked liked but without the low cut hair. It's the green dress I think that takes precedence in this dream and the dark skin.*

This black woman was working and or cleaning up these other souls (dead people) and this white woman that supposedly worked in this funeral home and or dead house could not go in; she was being locked out; barred from entering the area where these other people; souls and or spirits were.

*If any of you know the spiritual realm, you know that in order to cross over to the realm of truth you have to be changed; cleaned up. It's like an operation that you get. Well we see it as an operation. **Thus many black churches use to sing this song called; WE SHALL BE CHANGED, CHANGED FROM MORTAL TO IMORTALITY IN A TWINKLING OF AN EYE. This song is true to the spirit and the spiritual changes good and true people must go through before they get to Lovey.***

So with her showing me that she is being locked out means to me that; YOU WHITE PEOPLE BASED ON HUE AND YES DEEDS INCLUDING ANCESTRAL SINS THAT ARE LEFT UNPAID; YOU ARE BEING LOCKED OUT OF LOVEY'S REALM AND ABODE; KINGDOM. THUS THE LOCK OUT FOR YOU THE WHITE RACE IN SKIN TONE; HUE AND DEEDS

HAS AND HAVE BEGUN. YOU ARE BEING REJECTED AND NOT ONE OF YOU CAN DO OR SAY OTHERWISE BECAUSE THE NASTY HISTORY OF YOU AND WHAT YOUR RACE HAS AND HAVE DONE TO HUMANITY GLOBALLY IS ON RECORD FOR ALL TO SEE AND READ.

So truly good luck to your race because you all will have hell to pay shortly for your wrongs.

Lovey did not give you his strength or power, thus Zion now resides with the Chinese because they did accept the Ying and Yang; Life as we know it and death as we know it also.

They have the march of Zion and it is now up to them to truly trample down the beast in goodness and in truth. Yes revelations must be fulfilled in regards to Nimrod; sin and death. Thus England and many European Nations will never ever be the same. He who Satan gave his power to must sit on the throne of England and bring the global empires that he now owns back to India.

He cannot bring it to Ethiopia. He could but he cannot. India must get the devil's power because this is the land of Satan's birth. Thus every man of sin including your so called Jesus had to go into this land in the days of old to learn how to manipulate and deceive; thus the religions of man; men until this day. Say because I truly do not care what you say. You have the truth and you have the bible to back it up. No Indian can say otherwise because like I said, none is found on the Mountain of God; Good God and Allelujah; Lovey. They are of Babylon by DEATH AND DESCENT. This is the way I saw it and this is the way I am relating it back to you. So go ahead call me a racist and a liar then turn around and call Lovey a racist and a liar also if you dare. Like I said, this is how I saw it and this is how I am relating it back to you.

The lies of man and men must stop. Thus Vatican; the Vatican, which is the house of the dead must go down in flames also for the lies and deceit they spread. You cannot rob humanity of their soul and or spirit and expect Lovey to be with you. ***Death is with you so YOU LIE TO PEOPLE AND TELL THEM THAT YOU CAN FORGIVE THEIR SINS WHEN YOU KNOW THAT YOU CANNOT.***

NO MAN CAN FORGIVE ANOTHER FOR THEIR SINS IF THAT PERSON DID NOT ERR YOU. NOT EVEN GOD; LOVEY HIMSELF CAN DO THIS. BUT YET EACH AND EVERY DAY YOU DARE PUT YOURSELF ABOVE LOVEY WITH YOUR LIES AND BULLSHIT; DECEIT. HELL IS THERE, THUS ALL OF YOU ARE TRULY CONDEMNED TO HELL FOR THE LIES YOU TELL AGAINST LOVEY.

England and you White People; the eye water of many did catch you including certain parts of Africa because Africa is also to blame for slavery (human trafficking) thus Mother Africa is tiad a di liads dem wey live inna har.

She is fed up of her own lying and deceiving people and the bullshit that they do. Thus humans globally are going to die because THIS IS TRULY THE END OF TIME.

So no matter how you leaders globe trot and promise; your deceit and lies cannot save you because they are recorded and one by one condemnation is falling on the lots of you including your land. Instead of saving self and land and making true peace; you all lie because your lands are bankrupt and slated to fall. So whatever you can do to take other lands with you to hell the lots of you are going to do.

Black People wake up BECAUSE BLOOD IS ON AND IN THE HANDS OF THESE LEADERS THAT HAVE AND HAS DECEIVED YOU. They must go down to hell; so now they are coming around with their offers that offends not only me but those that are in the spiritual realm. BOB MARLEY TOLD YOU AND OR US IN THE BEGINNING OF AMBUSH IN THE NIGHT HOW THEY WOULD COME AROUND TO DECEIVE YOU. BUT WE AS A PEOPLE AND NATIONS OF PEOPLE REFUSE TO SEE AND COMEPREHEND THE TRUTH. Like he said, we are too ignorant; thus your so called holy bible called us STIFF NECKED. Meaning we cannot hear, nor can we listen.

We as blacks have the truth but refuse to live by the truth. So yes I am fucking fed up of us period because we too fool fool sometimes.

It's a shame and pity that none of you can see this. So England keep your dog change because it is spit upon. Don't embarrass black people anymore because **NO BLACK PERSON GLOBALLY IS EMBARRASSING YOU AND YOUR LAND BY OFFERING YOU WORSE THAT DOG CHANGE AS AN OFFERING.**

Respect is due SO KEEP YOUR PRISON BULLSHIT AND HANDLE YOUR OWN AFFAIRS. Don't pawn them off on Jamaica. **Until you England and the world can respect BLACK PEOPLE AND OTHERS; THERE WILL BE NO PEACE BECAUSE PEACE AND TRUTH IS TRULY NOT IN ANY OF YOU. YOU ARE ALL LIARS AND DECEIVERS THAT TROT THE GLOBE LOOKING FOR YOUR NEXT VICTIMS TO PREY ON.**

You treat your dogs better than you treat other humans and now YU A CUM SPIT INNA DI BLACK MAN FACE AGAIN.

WAS YOUR FOREFATHERS HAND IN THE BUYING AND SELLING (HUMAN TRAFFICKING) OTHERWISE CALLED SLAVERY NOT ENOUGH?

Your land bought and sold human beings for profit and England did profit off the backs of Black People for you now to go to Jamaica and spit in the people's face with your $25 million dollar bullshit money to build a prison on the land. Fuck you and fuck England with your bullshit.

TREAT PEOPLE LIKE HUMAN BEINGS. YOU WOULD NOT LIKE IT IF SOMEONE DID THIS TO ENGLAND. SO WHY SHOULD BLACK PEOPLE AND OR THE PEOPLE OF THE CARIBBEAN LIKE IT?

Keep your disgrace money that is worse than a handout. Use it to buy toilet paper if it can for the people of England.

Do not disrespect because no one is disrespecting you. Do right if you are doing right.

And yes, I know you are not going to like these words but it needed to be said. YOU MADE ME HOLD MY HEAD DOWN IN SHAME AND DISGRACE FOR YOUR ACTIONS AND LACK OF TRUTH. Black People are not second class citizens that you can continue to feed the shit that comes out of your ass.

THIS IS WHY I AM SO FUCKING MAD AT THE BLACK RACE. IT'S PEOPLE, RACIST FACIST LIKE YOU THAT CAN COME INTO BLACK LANDS WITH

SHIT AND THEY GOBBLE IT UP WHIST THINKING THE SHIT YOU GIVE THEM FI NYAM A GOOD FOOD. Enough is fucking enough. Keep your prison. Why the hell should Jamaica house your criminals?

Are they all Jamaicans?

I guess and bet not.

The money that you are shelling out so, use it to help your people create jobs. Help the needy with their housing needs and so forth, but don't continue to insult and belittle the intelligence of Black People because many of us truly do not want your so called hand out and blood money; pittance of shit that can't help them.

Some may want it and that's truly a crying shame. An look wey yu guh with your jail bullshit. Jamaica.

Yu caane guh to other Caribbean islands with your jail bullshit, but yu guh a Jamaica.

Wow and dem di fool fool government a Jamaica let yu in an nuh run yu.

Only in Jamaica thus nothing surprises me with these people. Dem sell out Gad suh dem wi du anything fi a bag a rice to claate.

Hand out, hand out
Food fi gold (shit)
Hand out, hand out
Come get yu hand out

Bulla cake dey
Yu name write pan eee

Eee free

All yu affi du a sell mi yu land an people aunda di quiet.
No one needs to know

Hand out, hand out
Come get yu free food because mi noa unnu a all eediat
wey caane read or write; nor do you have any sense.

Come on monkeys
Come on coons
Niggers let's go
Join the line
I'm your saving grace
Worship me
Accept me because I am there for you.

Damn fools.

Michelle Jean

Thus black people wake up and live not die come on now.

People like Bob Marley and Marcus Mosiah Garvey including Lovey (who is spirit and not a person) cannot keep educating you for the better and you keep refusing.

I am tired of the lies and bullshit.

Lovey keep giving you things the soft and subtle way but I can't. I have to stir your spirit and get you to think and it matters not if you hate me.

I have to show you things the harsh way. Just as how my children have to learn the harsh way soon.

Life isn't about death, it's about life and you have to live your life. THERE IS NO LIFE IN DEATH, SO THINK AND LIVE WISE AND TRUE.

And White People based on hue and deeds truly think and look at the history of the White Race throughout history and tell me was your actions justified?

Are your actions justified today?
Is your hatred and racist nature justified when it comes to hue and or skin colour?

THUS NOT ALL WHITES FALL UNDER THE BANNER OF WHITE. SOME ARE BLACKS, THUS THEY FALL UNDER THE BLACK BANNER OF LOVEY; GOOD GOD AND ALLELUJAH.

*Yes some of you are being locked out but she was not clean in deed and hue. **A person that has more sin on his or her slate will not see life when the spirit sheds the flesh.** Remember, she reminded me of the PnG lady thus telling me she was not a good person and or spirit and because of this, she could not be let in.*

I've told you time and time again in my other books, THE LIFE YOU LIVE HERE ON EARTH DETERMINES WHERE YOU GO IN THE AFTER LIFE AND OR ONCE YOUR SPIRIT SHEDS THE FLESH. SO TRULY KNOW YOUR SINS AND TRY TO AMEND THEM. Meaning do the good that you can so that you are saved and safe in the spiritual realm.

The fire of our sun is not as hot as spiritual fire. Your spirit can go through the fire of our sun and live, but it cannot go through hell's fire because that fire was especially designed for you by you here in the living.

Your spirit have no say in death, but it has all the say here on earth and or in the living.

Michelle Jean

Yes it's October 07, 2015 and I am so finished editing and writing this book.

Also check out my novels that are available on Lulu and Amazon.com.

Here's a list of some of them.

Jamaican Tsunami
Heaven's Gate
A Thin Line Between Love And Hate
The Dark Side Of Love
Blind Obsession
Bodaciously You
Kane and Nubia
Book Of Short Stories

I keep wanting to do more for this line (romance line) of books but can't for some strange reason. I guess I have to complete the Michelle Jean line of books first.

At any rate stay safe and truly learn to live.

Oh, music.

*Check out these songs **by Ding Dong.***
Love Mi Nuh
Syvah
Way Up Stay Up

And **Gas.**

Trabass who is a You Tuber turned musician has a song out called Us featuring Alexus Rose. This girl can sing. Trabass yu a try doa an mi haffi rate you fi yu efforts.

Kicking it old school you have to check out:

BOUNCE by Red Fox.

HANDLE THE RIDE and BIG NINJA BIKE by Tanya Stephens.

So until book 23 people.

Walk and live, not walk and die.

Michelle

OTHER BOOKS BY MICHELLE JEAN

Blackman Redemption – The Fall of Michelle Jean
Blackman Redemption – After the Fall Apology
Blackman Redemption – World Cry – Christine Lewis
Blackman Redemption
Blackman Redemption – The Rise and Fall of Jamaica
Blackman Redemption – The War of Israel
Blackman Redemption – The Way I Speak to God
Blackman Redemption – A Little Talk With Man
Blackman Redemption – The Den of Thieves
Blackman Redemption – The Death of Jamaica
Blackman Redemption – Happy Mother's Day
Blackman Redemption – The Death of Faith
Blackman Redemption – The War of Religion
Blackman Redemption – The Death of Russia
Blackman Redemption – The Truth
Blackman Redemption – Spiritual War
Blackman Redemption – The Youths
Blackman Redemption – Black Man Where Is Your God?

The New Book of Life
The New Book of Life – A Cry For The Children
The New Book of Life – Judgement
The New Book of Life – Love Bound
The New Book of Life – Me
The New Book of Life – Life

Just One of Those Days
Book Two – Just One of Those Days
Just One of Those Days – Book Three The Way I Feel
Just One of Those Days – Book Four

The Days I Am Weak
Crazy Thoughts – My Book of Sin
Broken
Ode to Mr. Dean Fraser

A Little Little Talk
A Little Little Talk – Book Two

Prayers
My Collective
A Little Talk/A Time For Fun and Play
Simple Poems
Behind The Scars
Songs of Praise And Love

Love Bound
Love Bound – Book Two

Dedication Unto My Kids
More Talk
Saving America From A Woman's Perspective
My Collective the Other Side of Me
My Collective the Dark Side of Me
A Blessed Day
Lose To Win
My Doubtful Days – Book One

My Little Talk With God
My Little Talk With God – Book Two

A Different Mood and World – Thinking

My Nagging Day

My Nagging Day – Book Two
Friday September 13, 2013
My True Love
It Would Be You
My Day

A Little Advice – Talk
1313, 2032, 2132 – The End of Man
Tata

MICHELLE'S BOOK BLOG – BOOKS 1 – 21

My Problem Day
A Better Way
Stay – Adultery and the Weight of Sin – Cleanliness
Message

Let's Talk
Lonely Days – Foundation
A Little Talk With Jamaica – As Long As I Live
Instructions For Death
My Lonely Thoughts
My Lonely Thoughts – Book Two
My Morning Talks – Prayers With God
What A Mess
My Little Book
A Little Word With You
My First Trip of 2015
Black Mother – Mama Africa
Islamic Thought
My California Trip January 2015
My True Devotion by Michelle – Michelle Jean
My Many Questions To God

My Talk

My Talk Book Two

My Talk Book Three – The Rise of Michelle Jean

My Talk Book Four

My Talk Book Five

My Talk Book Six

My Talk Book Seven

My Talk Book Eight – My Depression

My Talk Book Nine – Death

My Talk Book Ten – Wow

My Day – Book Two

My Talk Book Eleven – What About December?

Haven Hill

What About December – Book Two

My Talk Book Twelve – Summary and or Confusion

My Talk Book Thirteen

My Talk Book Fourteen – My Talk With God